"Insider Secrets of How to Buy and Sell Custom and Classic Cars" For Profit

Tips, Tricks and Secrets to Buying Low and Selling High

Lance Von Prum, author

Copyright 2013

Second edition; October 24, 2014

Table of Contents

Introduction

Introduction

With over thirty-five years experience in the custom car industry, starting in Southern California, I've seen it all. From working on the flying car in the movie, "Bladerunner" to a building a Rolls Royce stretch limo, I've gotten quite a broad look inside many different aspects of the "Custom" car industry, including concept cars, convertible conversions, restorations, one-of-a-kind cars, and every now and then, a real 40's or 50's custom car or hot rod. Since then, I've worked on hundreds of cars, mostly 30's, 40's, 50's, 60's and 70's cars and trucks, either restored or customized or both.

Each Car has a different story to tell and each car owner has many stories to tell, some good stories and some that range from headaches to continuing nightmares. I've seen this all too often. I've seen what looked like a fairly good car, turn out to be a rusted out hulk under some shiny paint and plastic filler. There are good cars out there, and I've written this series of eBooks to help custom car lovers get more enjoyment out of their cars, fewer headaches and no nightmares. Each eBook explores a different aspect of custom car ownership with the focus on helping out you car guys young and old make good decisions that maximize enjoyment and control expenses.

My apologies to the ladies who read this and don't feel like a "car guy." I understand, but this hobby is 95 percent male, and the other 5 percent are married to car guys. If I am wrong, you ladies let me know and we'll start a "gals cars" page or something.

My sincere thanks to Gene Winfield for seeing something special in me and drawing it out. Gene is a very special guy.

I thank every one of my instructors at The Art Center College of Design in Pasadena, California for teaching me to see what I'm looking at, to understand what I see and reproduce it.

Thanks go to many others but a special thanks goes to my friend Philip Mesa, without whose help I could not have done this.

"Insider Secrets of How to Buy and Sell Custom and Classic Cars For Profit"

Charter 1

This Is a Risky Business

A car is only worth what someone will pay for it, and right now people are holding on to their money, uncertain about the future, but many are not holding on to their custom cars. Some don't want to sell because the market is depressed, but others are selling for a variety of reasons. Some of these reasons are hardships and lifestyle changes. Unfortunate for the seller but good for you, but how do you know if the price is a good deal?

If you ask three knowledgeable custom car guys what a certain car is worth, you'll get three different prices. So, you might think that you are buying a custom car at a low price, only to learn that you can't sell it for what you paid for it. If you think you've bought a car right and keep it for a while, the market may change, and you know Murphy's Law, the value probably won't go up. Don't let this discourage you. You just need to do your homework and educate yourself before you go looking at cars or plunking down any cash.

You really have to know your cars. A 57 Chevy, two door, Bel Air Sedan is worth less than a 57 Chevy Bel Air hardtop. 70's muscle cars are tricky. Some  aren't worth a lot, while others are skyrocketing in value. A 32 Ford roadster can be worth twice what a 31 Ford roadster in equal condition is worth. You really have to know your stuff and then still do a lot of homework to keep from buying the wrong car, or paying the wrong price.

Whether you are new to custom and classic cars or an old timer at this game, you need to be current with your information. Prices on most cars have fallen, but some have gone up in value. Don't assume you know your stuff when it comes to handing over a big stack of greenbacks. Search the Internet, join car blogs, check craigslist and see what's out there. You can't know too much.

Chapter 2

Which Car to Buy?

You're buying this car to sell, so you want to buy a popular car. So what is popular? Fads come and go. 32 Fords were hot until they got so dang expensive that now no one wants to risk owning one, while over-inflated values decline. 1955, 56, 57 and 58 Chevy's have always been popular, but are hard to buy cheap. I said hard, not impossible because there are lots of them. These cars are practically indestructible and have survived better than most.

The 70's muscle cars are good choices. Popularity for these cars is growing. There are still lots of them left and good deals are fairly easy to find, because values are going up on a lot of these cars, and not everybody knows it.

Although not necessarily a custom car, Volkswagens are a good bet. If your budget is on the low end of the spectrum you couldn't go wrong with a Bug. Lots of cars, lots of parts and lots of people want them. Volkswagen buses are also popular and more practical,

especially the window vans, especially the twenty-three and twenty-five window vans. A good price on one of these will be hard to come by, but not impossible.

You can still find mid-60's Chevy II's and Malibu's on the road in original condition, and there are tons of aftermarket parts available for these cars. Ford Falcons are popular and not too hard to find. There are plenty of new reproduction parts available for these as well.

There is no end to the good cars out there. Project cars are a good possibility. These cars are unfinished cars started by

someone, and are now for sale for a number of reasons. Divorce seems to top the list, then comes the lost job and need the money for something else. You can get some good deals here, even pennies on the dollar, but then you have to finish the car to get top dollar, which means that you need a shop, or you have to pay someone to finish the car. It will be hard to make a profit this way unless you buy the car for next to nothing. The best project car for our purposes is one that's almost done and only needs a few things to complete.

Trucks are very popular. There are plenty good trucks from the 50's, 60's and 70's out there, as well as good parts availability. Stick with Fords and Chevy's. The Dodges don't have near the popularity right now. Trucks have a following of their own, and a good deal on an old truck is probably easier to find than on most other cars. Trucks are utilitarian, and the owner of an old truck won't care too much about a scratch in the bed. He's using the truck to haul stuff and expects a little wear and tear.

If you are doing this to make a profit while playing with old cars, then it's really not too important exactly which vehicle you buy, as long as it is something mainstream. Focus on the good deal, rather than the type of vehicle you like most, because you're not going to keep it. So let's talk about the good deal.

Chapter 3

Finding a good deal

The big secret is, not to sell for a high price, but to buy at a low price and sell for fair market value. You're probably going to look at a lot of cars before you find a really good deal, because good deals are few in number, and they don't last long, but they are out there. You've got to find the guy in the middle of a divorce or he needs to make his child support payments, or has medical bills, or just a guy who does not value his car that much, or does not know the value of his car.

As you drive around, watch for old cars that aren't even for sale. If you see an old car, you might stop and ask if the owner would consider selling it. Often this situation can lead to a bargain deal.

To get a good deal on a car, you have to know what a good deal is. So, you found a car on craigslist and you've made arrangements to go look at the car. Before you head out the door, get on line and do a search for similar vehicles nationwide to get a range of prices.

Check prices with "Hemmings Motor News." Buy a copy at the book store and keep it on hand for reference. Buy a new issue every few months, because the market changes. They have tons of listings in every category every month. You can also go on line to their web site to check prices. Here's the link: http://www.hemmings.com.

Remember that the asking price is seldom the selling price. Generally, cars sell for ten percent or more below the asking price, so use the ten percent number. Condition is everything. The condition of the car is the largest factor determining its value. Read the descriptions of the cars you've found and only use the numbers from the cars that best match the description of the one you are about to look at in person.

If the car you found on craigslist is unrestored, don't look at restored car prices, and think you've found a good deal. Find the closest matches that you can, to make your comparisons. If your craigslist car is at or near the bottom of your pricing search, then there is a chance you have found a good deal. Make a list, or better yet, print out the listings you've found online, and bring them with you. Now you are ready to go look at the car.

Chapter 4

What to Look For

You're doing this to make money, so you don't want just any car that is priced low. What you *do* want is a car others will want, a car with potential. You're doing this to make a profit, so you don't want to own this car a long time. A car with potential is one that you can put a few dollars into, and make nicer, increasing its value and desirability. You want a car that you can improve without the need for a shop and a lot of tools, things you can do in your garage at home.

First and foremost, you want a car with a decent paint job. You don't want to repaint a car, so walk away from any car that has a lot of paint issues or has primer on part or all of it. Whether it's original paint or a repaint, get a car that you can wax up and will look acceptable.

You also don't want a car with rust issues. Rust repairs are very expensive. Lots of old cars have rust issues, but many don't, so look for rust in the usual places, down low behind the wheel wells and rocker panels, the bottoms of the doors and the bottom edge of the trunk

lid. If you discover rust damage, walk away. You don't want a rust damaged car, even if it is dirt cheap. I suggest you read my eBook, "Secrets of How to Get The Best Deal On A Custom Car" for a detailed description of what to look for. Find it, and my other custom car eBooks on Amazon.

What you are looking for is a car that is in relatively good shape, but has room for improvement in areas that you can do at home. A new carpet kit, for example is something relatively inexpensive and something you can do on a Saturday. Carpet kits are available for a large number of old cars, and require only a few hand tools. A new carpet really spruces up the interior. Cracked or fogged glass is relatively easy to deal with and not expensive. A car with missing or damaged parts might be a good choice if you know the parts are available and not expensive, but don't assume. Do your research before you buy the car.

In general, you want a relatively clean car that you can make better in a short period of time. You don't want to rebuild an engine or install a new transmission, but you can detail the engine compartment and install some new chrome plated or finned aluminum valve covers. These relatively inexpensive upgrades are eye catchers to your potential buyer.

So, as you look at a potential car to buy, think like the buyer you hope to sell to. He wants a really clean car with few issues and lots of potential, from his point of view. Your buyer wants a reliable car to drive, or a car that can be fully restored or made into a custom car. The car you want to buy is one that you can take to the next level and raise the value enough to make a modest profit. You also want a car with a clean title, so ask about the title in your email exchange or telephone call, before you go to look at a car. A car with no title or a bank lien is a problem you don't want.

Chapter 5

Making the Deal

You've finally found a car that you want to buy and you're ready to negotiate. As you looked at the car, you asked a lot of questions to  get a feel for the seller and the car. One question to ask is why he wants to sell the car. Whatever the answer, don't necessarily believe anything the seller says. You are just getting all the information you can, to get the best overall understanding of the situation. You should try to be as reputable as possible, but the seller may not be thinking the same way.

There are lots of horror stories of hidden rust, motors full of oil additives and transmissions that blow ten miles down the road. The more questions you ask, the better feel you get for both the car and the seller.

When you've made your decision and are ready to negotiate, tell the seller that you like the car, but there are issues. You should write these down as you look at the car and then refer to your list as you tell the seller that you'll have to spend more money to make the car right for you. Maybe it needs new tires or the battery is old and tired. Whatever, these are negotiating points to justify a lower offer. Mention every little thing you find, expressing some doubt in your voice. Even if the seller lowers the price, you stick to your guns and offer a lower price. How much lower is up to you, but the lower you go, meeting half way to close a deal only benefits you.

I'd suggest offering about twenty-five percent less than his last offer, saying that the car needs a lot of work to bring it up to snuff, and a lot of expense, because this is most often true. Then it might be worth what he's asking, but right now, that's where you stand. This will probably surprise the seller a bit, but you continue to justify your position. Remind him that the market for old and custom cars is in a slump, and people just aren't buying. Explain that cars like this have no fixed value, and it is only worth what someone is willing to pay, then up your price a little. You shouldn't lie, but you can be ruthless.

You may get the seller to come down some more, or you may not. Every deal is different, and every seller is different. Your deal won't play out just as I've described, so use my tips as guidelines, tools to use as the situation dictates. Just do your best to get the lowest price you can, and be ready to walk if there is not enough profit in the deal.

If you will have to buy a set of tires, a carpet kit and search the Internet for an arm rest and a taillight, those expenses have to be recovered when you sell the car, plus some profit. So, you have to be able to think on your feet and factor your expenses to know what to pay. Be ready to walk away from a good car if you are the least bit uncertain. Often as not, this car will still be available a week or a month from now.

Never let your emotions enter into the picture. You might begin to think that you may not find another deal like this, or you can't wait to drive it after you fix it up. This is a business deal, so don't let yourself start thinking like a teenager.

Chapter 6

Closing the Deal

All right! You finally found a good car at the right price. Have the cash ready. No checks. Sellers don't like checks, and a big stack of cash is motivating to the seller. You might have a blank bill of sale prepared, or ask the seller to write a bill of sale. Make sure the title is clear, not a branded title, which means that the car was wrecked and rebuilt. Make sure the title is in the seller's name. You don't want a title that the previous owner signed off, but the current owner never registered. You will see this a lot with old and classic cars, so if the title is already signed but not dated, verify the seller's identity. Make sure the seller is the legal owner.

Now, ask him to sign the title but not date it, and the same for the bill of sale. You can tell him that you are buying the car to resell, but you have to put time and more money in it before you do. Most people understand this and won't care. They just want to see the car go away and put the money in their pocket.

Depending on what state you are in, this practice of holding a title is technically illegal, unless you are a car dealer, so do some homework here, because you don't want to register the car in your name unless you have to, and if you do this several times, your state may require you to get a dealer's license. As a general rule most states allow you thirty days to register a vehicle. If you can turn the vehicle in that time, you shouldn't have a problem. If you can get the seller to not date the title and bill of sale, then you can stretch that thirty day time period.

When you go to sell this car, you simply explain to your buyer, that you are in the business of buying and selling cars, and most buyers will understand. This is kind of a gray area, so check with your state on their dotgov web site. Unless you buy and sell fifty cars a year you should be all right.

Bring a friend with you, or your wife, so you can drive your new purchase home. If you are uncertain about the car, trailer it. If you have a car trailer, never bring it with you to look  at a car. That tells the seller that you expect to buy the car and he probably won't negotiate as much. Call your buddy and have him bring the truck and trailer after the sale, or call a towing company. If you do this several times a year, you can usually make a deal with smaller towing companies to give you a better price. I would not recommend leaving the car once you have paid for it.

Chapter 7

Now It's Yours, What to Do

You want to turn this car as soon as possible for maximum profit, so first, determine what you intend to do to the car and what you expect to sell the car for. This will help you monitor and control your budget. If you paid $10,000 for a car and expect to sell it for $15,000, then don't spend more than a grand or fifteen hundred bucks fixing it up. You may only get twelve, but if you've done good research, you'll get fourteen or fifteen grand.

The first step is to clean the thing, top to bottom. Go to the "Do it yourself" car wash, or use a pressure washer to get the grease and road grime off the underside and engine compartment. Get the dirt and gunk out of the trunk and wheel wells. Get some polishing compound and see if you can't get a little more shine out of the paint and chrome. Detail the engine compartment, noting anything you want to replace along the way.

Think like a buyer and do all you can to overcome any objections a buyer might find. Everything you don't do will become an issue when you are selling. So make sure you start with a car that will have no serious issues when you are done, and you will end up with a very desirable car that is easy to sell for top dollar.

You'll want to replace anything that's worn or broken, plus anything that will help improve the overall appearance of the car without a large expense. New hoses and belts are inexpensive and are sure to catch your buyer's eye. Finned aluminum valve covers are a good example of a nice dress-up item that will help make a better first impression. Try to find them cheap on craigslist or at a swap meet.

Take the wheels off and check the brakes. Replace the brake shoes as needed and look for leaky wheel cylinders. Replace those if necessary, then flush out the old brake fluid, put in new fluid and bleed the brakes. Check the wheel bearings and ball joints or kingpins. Are the tires good? Even if they are fifty percent, consider putting on a new set of tires. It's a good selling point, and you are turning a negative into a positive. Depending on the car or truck, you might consider a set of alloy wheels. Don't buy these new. Find a nice set on craigslist for a couple hundred bucks and throw 'em on. Try to buy all your dress-up items used and keep your expenses down.

Now you know the car is safe to drive, but you should change the oil and coolant if the previous owner didn't. Unleaded fuel is hard on old gas tanks, so drain the fuel, drop the tank and flush it out. If you find a lot of rust but the tank is not leaking, seal it with a good fuel tank sealer like POR15. Seal the fuel line pick up with a plug or a golf tee and the filler neck and fuel tank sending unit hole with duct tape, then pour in the sealer and slosh the stuff around to get every square inch inside covered. Then drain the excess and let the tank dry for a few days and reassemble everything. Replace the fuel filter or put one in line if there isn't one, and you how have a safe and dependable car with very little expense. You can do all of this for a hundred dollars or so and although not visible, is a good selling point. Be sure to include this on your list of repairs and upgrades to show your prospective buyer.

Focus on what will make the car look better for the least expense. If the seats are worn, ripped and torn, pre-sewn seat cover kits are available for a lot of the more popular cars, are quite affordable, and easy to install yourself. A broken or fogged window is no big deal. All the side windows in the older cars are flat glass, are inexpensive and relatively easy to replace.

If you bought a custom car, or want to take the first steps to turning an old car into a custom, there are thousands of dress-up items that you can bolt on, but before you start buying a string of shiny objects, consider a theme. Things should match, compliment each other and go well together. Think this through and be selective about your choices. You don't want to spend money that you don't have to. Although you may like something, this may actually narrow your market when you are ready to sell. If a potential buyer doesn't like your choices, he won't buy your car, or want to pay a lot less. Look in magazines for ideas. Cars that make it into the magazines are usually the cream of the crop, so use magazine cars as a guide.

Fix everything that doesn't work. Whether it's a wiper motor, a fuel gauge or a speedometer, turn a negative into a positive. Whatever you do, document it. Take pictures and make a journal of all the repairs and upgrades, and save all the receipts. This adds value to your vehicle. You can show your prospective buyer what you have done and what you have spent as an aid to help support your asking price. You should tell your buyer that this documentation adds value to the car because you've documented every dime spent and all repairs made. Documentation reveals the hidden things you've done, like the new brakes and fuel tank seal.

Do all you can to add value to your car without investing a lot. Remember that your goal is to create a saleable car without breaking the bank. Use more labor than money. You want to make a profit, so don't spend money that doesn't need to be spent. Evaluate each expense. Does this expense turn a negative into a positive, or is it an expense that needn't be incurred? Invest your money wisely to maximize your profit. Remember that this is a risky business, so you have to think through every move you make.

Chapter 8

Now what?

Your car is done! It looks great, and you are ready to sell.   If you are web savvy, create a web site that

describes your car in detail with one large photo and several smaller ones. If you aren't web savvy, get your kid to do it for you, pay the neighbor kid a few bucks, or call your nephew. Use a cloud storage service like Dropbox or Google Drive, where you can upload as many photos as you want, along with your other receipts and documentation. Then add a link on your web site so people can learn more about the car.

Start with craigslist, because your buyer is most likely in your area, but try everything, because you never know. Lots of Internet sites are free to list your car. They make their money in other ways, so list with every one you can. Put emotion into your ads. Be proud of your car and let it show. This will increase interest. If you are dealing in high-end cars, you should seriously consider putting ads in magazines like "The Robb Report" and "The DuPont Register." Don't forget "Hemmings Motor News." I'd also strongly suggest an ad in the classified section of the Sunday edition of the Orange County Register newspaper. There's lots of money in Southern California, and lots of car enthusiasts.

Your initial ad should provide all the prominent information about your car but not too much. Most people won't read more than two or three sentences. Let your initial ad be the hook, and provide detailed information and photos upon request or through your web site. Photos say more than words, so take good photos and post as many as you can, two of the whole car, one of the interior and one of the engine compartment and any other strong feature your car may have is a minimum. A picture says a thousand words.

As you get responses to your ad, reply in a positive way, asking to set an appointment for a showing. Answer all questions honestly and suggest the interested party call you for more information. Don't appear desperate, but accommodating.

Chapter 8

Showing Your Car

You've set an appointment to show your car. You want to show it in a positive setting, so clean up the garage, put all the tools away and sweep the floor. If it's a nice day, put the car in your driveway. Dress clean and casual, be upbeat and put on your best game face. As you show the car, point out all of its positive features. Show your documentation to your potential buyer and tell him about things that are not obvious such as a

cleaned and sealed gas tank, rebuilt front suspension or new brakes. Answer all of your buyer's questions with a positive point of view.

Let your potential buyer drive the car, but go with him. Never let anyone drive your car without you, especially if it is a high performance car. When you go along for the ride, you can continue to point out the car's good points, like how well it handles, or how quiet it is, or how loud it is.

You've dealt with all the car's issues so you can tell your buyer that the car needs nothing. Make a big deal of this. How many old cars don't need anything? After the drive, if your potential buyer is interested, he'll make you an offer. Never accept the first offer unless it is a full price offer. Tell your buyer again that the car needs nothing, and that you have priced it at fair market value, explaining again how you arrived at that number. Don't give a counter-offer. Let the buyer do that. Everyone expects to negotiate, so be prepared to come down a little, and have that number in your head. Price your car a little above what you will accept. Have a number that you will settle for and no less. Don't cave in because you have a legitimate buyer. You're in this to make a profit.

Let your buyer walk if he won't meet your price. It's not about selling a car, it's about getting your price. If you have a nice car, you will have lots of traffic, so just wait for the next guy.

Chapter 9

The Close, Wrapping Up the Deal

 You may show your car a half dozen or more times or more before it sells, but remember, you are trying to get the top end of the current market value, or a little more. Remember also that these cars don't have a bluebook value. They are worth what someone is willing to spend. If you do decide to lower your price, keep the phone numbers of previous lookers so you can call and offer your reduced price.

Be passionate about your car! Emotion sells! Make your prospective buyer fall in love with your car. Don't just show your car, really sell it! Explain all that you've done, that the buyer won't have to. Show him the photos and the receipts for all that you have done. Remind the buyer how hard it is to find a good clean car.

When you finally get a prospective buyer to agree to pay your price, congratulations! You've bought and sold a custom car for a profit! Date the title and the bill of sale and say goodbye to your car and its new owner. Now you're ready to repeat the process with experience under your belt! Nice going!

Chapter 10

Some Final Thoughts

Remember, there is a risk that you'll have paid too much, or can't sell the car for what you thought, so do your homework. I can't stress this enough. I sincerely want you to make a nice profit, and that can best be done with good, thorough research. Keep your emotions out of this. It's easy to get excited about a cool car, and that voice in your head starts telling you that you could pay a little more. This is business, so keep a cool head. If you do sense your emotions creeping in, tell the seller that you'll have to think about it. When you walk away from a car, you haven't lost anything, and the seller just may cave in as you start to leave.

Go to a coffee shop and think about it. Call a buddy and get some feedback. If you just can't decide, walk away. Even if you miss a good deal, you haven't lost anything. There are lots of other cars out there. It's not the only good deal, or the last one. Let a deal go rather than let your money go. Keep that in mind. You'll never regret it. You may look at lots of cars before you find the car and the deal you've been looking for.

I wish you the best of luck. Please give me your comments and feedback through Amazon. New and expanded information will be added to future editions to better help future readers. Please check out my other custom car books, also available on Amazon. I truly want to help you guys and gals enjoy your cars to the fullest, and avoid a lot of the headaches and nightmares that can and do happen. Keep the shiny side up!

Made in the USA
Columbia, SC
28 April 2022

59639385R00022